BLACKS IN AMERICA

ANN KRAMER

SEA-TO-SEA

Mankato Collingwood London

Illustrations   David Frankland

Designer   Billin Design Solutions
Editor   Penny Clarke
Art Director   Jonathan Hair
Editor-in-Chief   John C. Miles

This edition first published in 2005 by
Sea-to-Sea Publications
1980 Lookout Drive
North Mankato
Minnesota 56003

ISBN   1-932889-26-4

Printed in China

Library of Congress Control Number: 2004103721

2 4 6 8 9 7 5 3

Published by arrangement with the Watts Publishing
Group Ltd, London

CONTENTS

African Roots

Most black Americans trace their distant ancestry to a vast area in West Africa known as the western Sudan. There, from about A.D. 300, a number of wealthy and sophisticated kingdoms rose and fell.

"The Sultan of Mali holds audiences in the palace yard, where there is a platform, which they call the pempi. It is carpeted with silk and covered with cushions. Over it is raised the umbrella, a sort of pavilion of silk, at the top of which is a bird made from solid gold ... musicians walk in front of him, playing gold and silver instruments, and behind him walk 300 armed slaves."

Mohammad ibn Battuta, Muslim traveler c. 1350

GREAT KINGDOMS

The continent of Africa, where human beings originated, has an ancient history. Egypt, in northern Africa, was one of the most highly developed and influential societies of the ancient world.

By about A.D. 300 great kingdoms and cities had arisen in the part of Africa south of the vast Sahara Desert. The first of these kingdoms was Ghana, which lay along West Africa's Senegal and Niger Rivers.

The Ghanaians were the first in western Africa to smelt iron ore, producing iron weapons that helped them to conquer neighboring nations. Ghana became a powerful trading state with a huge army. Its wealth came from gold mines and trade with North Africa. Its scholars were skilled mathematicians and astronomers.

In the 11th century Muslims from Morocco invaded Ghana and the kingdom collapsed, to be replaced by the powerful kingdom of Mali. Under their ruler, Mansa Musa, the people of Mali created an advanced culture. The city of Timbuktu was a center of study, especially for law and Islamic studies.

Eventually Mali was succeeded by the Songhai Empire which, in its turn, became the most powerful kingdom in West Africa.

It set up universities in Timbuktu, Jenne, and elsewhere. These attracted scholars from Europe and Asia.

From the 15th century on it was Africans from these empires, and smaller kingdoms such as Dahomey, Benin, Kanem, and Ashante, who were transported as slaves to the Americas.

SLAVERY

Slavery—and the trade in slaves—existed in Africa well before the Europeans arrived. West African kingdoms traded gold and slaves with the Berbers of North Africa, whose merchants crossed the Sahara Desert carrying silk and other luxury goods. The Berbers also traded with Europe and Asia.

Slavery within African society was a way of life, similar to slavery in ancient Greece or Rome.

PRISONERS

Slaves were often prisoners of war, captured by advancing armies and either forced into military service or used as domestic servants. Sometimes destitute individuals sold themselves into slavery to avoid debt.

Some, but not all, slaves were sold to Arab traders for a profit. Conditions for slaves were often harsh, and slaves had no real rights. But slavery was often just a temporary punishment. After a considerable time slaves could usually obtain their freedom and become part of the community.

But all this was to change once the European traders arrived on the West African coast and established their own slave trade.

A fine bronze head from the African kingdom of Benin.

WEST AFRICAN CIVILIZATION

A.D. 610–733 Islamic faith spreads across northern Africa.

700–900 Berbers in North Africa set up trans-Saharan slave trade.

900–1250 Kingdom of Ghana is at its most powerful and trades with Berbers.

c. 1235–1500 Mali Empire flourishes. Founded by warrior king Sandiata, it reaches its peak under its great ruler Mansa Musa (ruled 1312–37). Wealth comes from gold mines and trade.

c. 1352 Arab traveler Ibn Battuta stays in Niani, the capital of Mali.

c. 1464 Songhai ruler and warrior king Sonni Ali (1464–92) conquers Timbuktu. Songhai Empire flourishes in former Mali territory until 1591.

Atlantic Slave Trade

In the 1400s Europeans arrived on the coast of West Africa looking for gold. They soon became involved in the African slave trade. Over the next hundred years they set up a brutal and profitable trade that would transport millions of Africans across the Atlantic to the Americas.

> **"They parted husbands from wives, fathers from sons, brothers from brothers."**
>
> **From a description of a Lagos slave auction**

FORCED MARCHES

The Portuguese arrived first. They set up trading posts and forts along the coast and began buying slaves from African merchants who brought captured slaves from the interior to the coast. Groups of up to 150 Africans, including Ibo, Ashante, and Fulani peoples, were chained together and marched long distances to European trading posts. There the European traders examined them and, if satisfied with their condition, bought them. Once purchased, the slaves were branded and imprisoned in the grim forts, often underground, waiting to be shipped across the ocean to the Americas.

THE MIDDLE PASSAGE

For those who survived the forced march and imprisonment, worse was to follow. Slaves were chained together and packed as tightly as possible into slave ships for the infamous Middle Passage across the Atlantic Ocean, a journey that could take 16 weeks.

Conditions on the slave ships, which the Portuguese called *tumbeiros* (coffins), were dreadful. The slaves were often packed into the holds on their sides to save space.

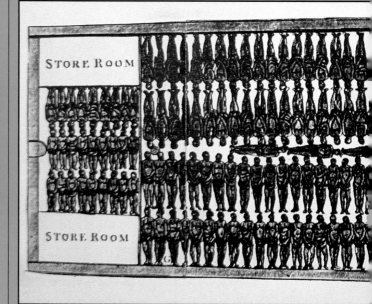

In the early years of the trade, 25 to 40 percent of the slaves died from disease and starvation. Some committed suicide by throwing themselves overboard.

"A MOST PROFITABLE TRADE"

The slave trade was highly profitable. Beginning in the 1500s, the Portuguese and Spanish colonized the Caribbean and what became known as Latin America. They set up plantations, worked by slave labor, to produce sugar, tobacco, and cotton—goods that sold for high prices in Europe. As native Americans died from disease, Europeans brought in slaves from West Africa.

By 1502 Portuguese traders were shipping West African people to Spanish and Portuguese colonies in the Caribbean and Brazil.

Within a few years the British, French, and Dutch had joined the trade. Traders in cities such as Bristol made fortunes as their ships sailed the so-called triangular trade routes.

The ships left Europe with goods such as guns, which were traded for slaves in Africa. Then, packed with human cargo, the ships crossed the Atlantic Ocean.

In the Caribbean the surviving slaves were sold. The ships then returned to Europe laden with goods, such as sugar and rum, for sale in European markets.

EARLY ATLANTIC SLAVE TRADE

1494 Treaty of Tordesillas divides New World between Portugal and Spain.

1502 Portuguese ships begin transporting West African slaves to the Americas.

1517 Spanish crown agrees that Spanish settlers should be allowed a regular supply of African slaves. Formal start of the Atlantic slave trade.

1518 Spanish King Charles V grants an *asiento* (commercial license) to individuals importing slaves into Spanish American colonies.

1562 Englishman John Hawkins organizes a trading voyage to Spanish colonies in the Caribbean. His ship carries goods from Europe and slaves he bought on the West African coast.

1600 About 900,000 enslaved Africans have been shipped to Latin America.

1655 Britain dominates slave trade.

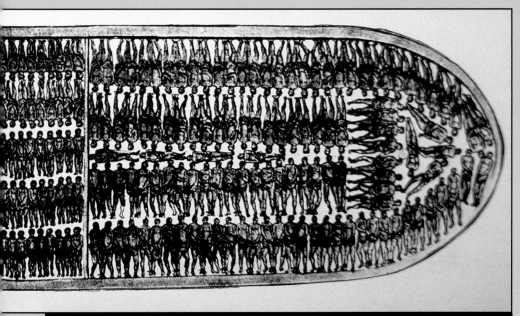

Conditions on slave ships were horrific, with humans packed in like stacked logs.

EQUIANO

Olaudah Equiano (1745–97) was born in a village in what is now Nigeria. He was captured by slave traders when he was 10 and transported to the Caribbean. He learned English and bought his freedom when he was 21.

He became active in the antislavery movement and published an account of his life: *The Interesting Narrative of the Life of Olaudah Equiano* (1789). It describes the horrors of the Middle Passage in minute detail.

Early Arrivals

In the 17th century alone some 2,750,000 Africans were shipped to the Americas—one of the largest forced migrations of people in history. Most went to the Caribbean, but from 1619 black Africans began arriving in the British colonies of North America.

> "... all negroes ... hereafter shall be bought and sold for slaves, are hereby declared slaves; and they, and their children, are hereby made and declared slaves."
>
> **Slave code, South Carolina, 1682**

A HUMAN FACTORY

As European countries scrambled for colonies in the "New World," thousands of slaves were imported to work plantations in Cuba, Jamaica, and Barbados. Boatloads of Africans were brought over to replace those who died from disease and the dreadful working conditions. The Caribbean effectively became a slave "factory," where slaves were broken in to plantation life.

Some survivors were shipped to British colonies in North America.

BRITISH NORTH AMERICA

The first Africans arrived in Jamestown, Virginia, in 1619 and were sold by auction as indentured servants, contracted to work without wages for up to seven years, after which they became free. Many poor whites came to North America in the same way.

Most Africans, however, were transported to the colonies as slaves, with no hope of freedom. Their lives depended on their destination. Virginia, Maryland, and the Carolinas were, like the Caribbean, plantation economies, which relied on slaves to be an unpaid labor force on the plantations or farms. By 1700 there were 23,000 slaves in the South, working ceaselessly.

By contrast, black people arriving in non-plantation colonies in the North, such as the Quaker colony of Philadelphia, or New Jersey or New York, were more likely to be indentured servants, artisans, or house servants for white masters and mistresses.

RACISM AND SLAVE CODES

Slave traders and owners justified slavery on the grounds of race. They argued that Africans were an inferior race, not entitled to any basic human rights. They saw Africans as property—an asset that could be bought and sold.

From this came a racial prejudice that spread throughout the colonies. Slaves had no human rights or dignity. Families were separated—parents were parted from children, brothers from sisters. Even their African names were replaced with European names.

In the mid-1600s the British colonies legalized slavery. Anyone who was a so-called Negro was a slave for life. Slave laws also stated that the children of slaves automatically became slaves. Once this happened, the North American slave trade grew more quickly.

Fearful of uprisings, such as those that had happened in the Caribbean, the British colonies introduced harsh slave "codes." These prohibited slaves from learning to read and write, carrying weapons, meeting in groups, or moving around without written permission.

FACT FILE

SLAVE REBELLIONS

Africans resisted slavery from the earliest days of the slave trade.

1522 Slaves rebel on the island of Santo Domingo.

1655 Black slaves in Jamaica, known as maroons, escape and set up free black communities in the mountains, where they maintain their African culture.

1673 Two hundred runaway slaves join the maroons.

1729 Led by Cudjoe, maroons fight British colonists in a successful guerrilla war lasting more than 10 years.

1791 Slaves stage unsuccessful uprising in Saint Dominique; their leader, Vincent Oge, is executed.

1791 In Haiti, Toussaint L'Ouverture leads army of slaves against French; rebellion lasts 13 years.

In America, slaves were auctioned like livestock. This illustration is from the 1850s.

Unequal Independence

Black slaves found strength in religious gatherings such as this prayer meeting.

In 1776 the 13 British colonies in North America staged a revolution and declared independence. A new nation independent of Britain was born: the United States of America. However, independence did not mean equality for African Americans.

"It has always appeared a most iniquitous scheme to me to fight ourselves for what we are daily robbing from those who have as good a right to freedom as we have."

Abigail Adams, wife of US President John Adams

TWO SOCIETIES

Two societies had emerged in the colonies. One was white and free, the other was black and mainly enslaved. By the mid-18th century there were more than 500,000 black people in the 13 colonies. Some were Africans who had been captured and brought to the colonies. Others, known as Creoles, had been born in the colonies. They drew on traditional African culture but supplemented it with their experience in the Americas, so marking the beginning of a distinctive, new African-American culture.

DECLARATION OF INDEPENDENCE

Tensions had developed between the white colonists and the British government. Some white colonists questioned Britain's right to tax them and began a move for independence.

WHEATLEY

Phillis Wheatley (c. 1753–84) is considered by many to be the first black American poet. She was born in Africa and taken to Boston as a slave when she was a child. She was bought by a tailor, John Wheatley, to be a servant for his wife. Unusually, the Wheatleys educated her. When she was 13 she began writing poetry; she published her first poem in 1770. In 1778 she gained her freedom.

In 1775 war broke out between Britain and its American colonies. The following year the Americans declared independence.

Hoping for their freedom, African Americans fought on both sides. Many black people, believing in the ideals of liberty described in the colonists' Declaration of Independence, fought with the colonists. Others sided with the British, who, in 1775, announced that any slave joining them would be given their freedom.

EMANCIPATION?
Fighting ended in 1781, with the colonists victorious. The Declaration of Independence had stated that "all men are created equal," but how far did it apply to black people? By and large, it did not.

Some former colonies passed manumission (freedom from slavery) laws. But the South insisted on maintaining slavery. As a result, most black people in the North were able to obtain freedom, but those in the South remained enslaved.

And in 1787 the American Constitution recognized slavery as legal.

BLACK INITIATIVES
Although most black people in the North were technically free, they were still considered racially inferior. The American Constitution defined a Negro as only three-fifths of a human being, and therefore less than equal.

As a result, black people began to set up their own institutions. They created businesses and started black-only churches and schools. One of the most important was the African Methodist Episcopal Church, set up in Philadelphia in 1790 by the Reverend Richard Allen, who had saved enough money to buy his freedom. Allen and the Reverend Absalom Jones also founded the Free African Society. In 1799 its members sent a petition to Congress demanding an end to the slave trade.

Life On The Plantations

The invention of the cotton gin in 1793 revolutionised cotton production. In America's Deep South, where cotton was wealth, the economy boomed. In 1860 some 1.8 million slaves toiled in the plantations picking a harvest worth $200 million.

> "... the fears and labors of another day begin; and until its close there is no such thing as rest ..."
>
> **Solomon Northrup, a free black man who was kidnapped in New York and sold into slavery for 12 years on a Louisiana plantation**

DEMAND GROWS

The hot, humid climate of the southern states was ideal for growing cotton. But picking the plant and separating the sticky seeds from the plant's fibers was a slow business.

Using the cotton gin, a slave could separate 50 times more raw cotton per day, and production soared. As exports grew, so too did the demand for slaves, particularly in Alabama, Georgia, and Mississippi.

Between 1793 and 1808, more than 250,000 slaves were taken to the USA before the trans-Atlantic slave trade was finally abolished. For slave owners, profits were high. In a good year, a planter might make $250 on the cost of keeping each slave.

FIELD AND HOUSE SLAVES

Some plantations were small, worked by only 20–30 field slaves.

Some were kidnapped from the North, but most were African.

Others were vast, worked by as many as 300 or 400 slaves. Field slaves worked from sunrise to sunset, planting, hoeing, weeding, picking, and preparing cotton. Work was hard and monotonous. White owners, or a black overseer, supervised the work. Slaves were whipped to make them work harder.

House slaves worked in the plantation owner's house and gardens.

Yoked or tied together to hinder escape, slaves head out for another day of back-breaking toil in the plantation's fields.

DOUGLASS

Frederick Douglass (1818–95) was a leading abolitionist. He was born a slave on a Maryland plantation. When he was very young he was separated from his mother. He saw many of his relatives sold to other plantations. He educated himself in secret.

In 1838 he escaped to New York, changing his name to Douglass. British abolitionists bought his freedom in 1846. Douglass worked passionately for the abolition of slavery, traveling to Europe to lecture on black civil rights. Back in the USA, he was later appointed to goverment office.

FACT FILE

SLAVE REBELLIONS

1739 Stono Rebellion, South Carolina. Slaves stage armed uprising. Eighty slaves and 20 whites are killed.

1800 Gabriel Prosser, a slave from Henrico County, Virginia, collects guns and swords for an armed uprising. Someone informs on him. Prosser and 34 others are hanged.

1822 Denmark Vesey, a freed slave working as a carpenter in South Carolina, plans to lead some 9,000 slaves in a bid for human rights. A house slave informs on him. Vesey and other leaders are executed. Four white men are imprisoned for helping Vesey.

1831 Nat Turner leads a slave uprising in Southampton County, Virginia. Rebels kill 60 white people in 24 hours, the bloodiest slave rebellion in US history. Turner and others are executed. The uprising makes Americans realize that slavery has become an issue that must be dealt with.

They ran the house, cooking, cleaning, and caring for the owner's children and family. Sometimes black women were raped by white men.

House slaves were distrusted by the field slaves because they lived closer to the master.

SLAVE QUARTERS

Slaves lived in small huts or shacks near their master's house. Most slept on the floor or on blankets on top of straw or cornhusks. Meager weekly food rations were provided: small amounts of pork or bacon, corn, sweet potatoes, and molasses. Each hut might contain an extended family—perhaps as many as eight people, from grandparents to grandchildren.

The family was a source of strength, but slave marriages were not recognized as legal; families were broken up when children were sold. Within their quarters, African Americans kept their religion, culture, and music alive. By the 1800s many black people integrated Christian worship into their daily lives.

Slaves found ways of resisting their situation. They ran away, worked slowly, and sometimes staged armed uprisings. Elsewhere, a powerful abolition movement was developing.

Abolitionists

By the 19th century, antislavery campaigners were working to help slaves escape and to bring an end to slavery. The issue would split the United States and ultimately lead to civil war.

> **"The greatest riches in all America have arisen from our blood and tears . . . but . . . while you keep us in bondage and treat us like brutes . . . we cannot be your friends . . ."**
> David Walker's *Appeal*, 1829

EARLY ABOLITIONISTS
In the 1680s Quakers in Pennsylvania condemned slavery on humanitarian grounds. Opposition to slavery developed rapidly in the North, where economic activity centered on small farms and industry. In the 1800s campaigning gathered momentum as free blacks and white campaigners demanded an end to slavery.

In 1831 a white reformer, William Lloyd Garrison, began to publish *The Liberator*, demanding immediate freedom for slaves. Two years later, the American Anti-Slavery Society was formed, with 60 white and 3 black members. By 1838 its membership had grown to over 250,000 people. Despite bitter and violent opposition by slaveholders in the South, and pro-slavery Northerners, abolitionism spread through the North.

BLACK CAMPAIGNERS
In 1827 the free black abolitionist newspaper *Freedom's Journal* appeared. One of its writers, David Walker, published an *Appeal* in 1829. In it he claimed that, because of slavery, African Americans were the "most wretched, degraded, and abject set of beings that ever lived."

As the campaign for abolition gathered momentum, former slaves such as Sojourner Truth published their life stories and went on speaking tours. Women were active in the movement; some, such as Lucretia Mott, also campaigned for women's rights. Abolitionist literature flooded the South; it included Harriet Beecher Stowe's *Uncle Tom's Cabin* (1852).

Escaped slaves walk to freedom on the "Underground Railroad."

THE UNDERGROUND RAILROAD

Abolitionists risked their lives to help slaves escape from the South, using an elaborate network of secret escape routes known as the Underground Railroad. Runaway slaves ("passengers") traveled at night for safety. They were accompanied by "conductors" from one "station" (stopping place) to another, where they hid during the day.

The escape routes stretched from the South to the free North and Canada.

Between 1830 and 1850 some 2,500 slaves "rode" to freedom each year. Harriet Tubman was a famous "conductor" who helped over 300 slaves to freedom.

COMPROMISES

From 1820 the US Congress passed various slavery laws, but most were compromises.

California entered the Union as a non-slave state, but other territories entered with no decision made. Laws about returning fugitive slaves contradicted each other.

Some abolitionists entered politics. They founded what was to be the antislavery Republican Party. But by 1860 slavery remained legal and opposition from Southern states was as powerful as ever.

FACT FILE

LEGAL LANDMARKS

1820 Missouri Compromise. Maine is admitted to the Union as a free, non-slave state; Missouri is admitted as a slave state. Slavery is banned in territory north of the 36°30′ parallel.

1842 US Supreme Court rules that state officials are not authorized to return fugitive slaves to the South.

1850 California enters the Union as a free state; other territories enter with no decision; fugitive law makes it a crime to help runaway slaves; they must be returned to the South.

1854 Kansas-Nebraska Act revokes Missouri Compromise; new territories must decide the question of slavery.

1857 Dred Scott Case: Scott, a former slave who had lived in free states, sues his former "master" for freedom. The US Supreme Court rules that blacks are not citizens and therefore cannot take a case to court. Missouri Compromise ruled unconstitutional.

TRUTH

Sojourner Truth (c. 1797–1883) was an abolitionist who also fought for women's rights. Born a slave, she was given the name Isabella Baumfree. Passed from one household to another, she finally ran away, became free, and took the name Sojourner Truth.

Believing God had called her, she spoke out against slavery. In Ohio in 1851 she made a famous speech, saying "Nobody ever helped me into carriages. . . . I have plowed and planted . . . and bore the lash as well . . . and aren't I a woman?"

The Civil War

In 1861 tensions between the slave-owning South and free-labor North erupted into civil war. Over 38,000 black people died in the fighting. War ended in 1865, with a Union victory and the end of slavery.

> **"Let the slaves and free colored people be called into service, and formed into a liberation army to march into the South and raise the banner of emancipation."**
>
> Frederick Douglass, 1861

"A HOUSE DIVIDED"

In 1860 Abraham Lincoln was elected US president. A Republican, he was elected on a platform of halting the expansion of slavery. By 1861 the US consisted of 19 states in which slavery was prohibited and 15 states where slavery was allowed.

The Southern states were determined to keep not only slavery, but also a very different lifestyle and culture from the North.

There were also tensions over whether federal or state governments should determine the rights of individual states.

In December 1860, South Carolina voted to leave the Union. Other Southern states followed, and by 1861 eleven slave-owning states had formed a Confederacy with its own constitution. In April 1861 Confederate troops fired on Fort Sumter, South Carolina, and war began.

BLACK INVOLVEMENT

Lincoln went to war to "restore the Union," but slavery soon became the main issue. When the war began, Northern blacks, seeing the war as a way of ending slavery, tried to join the Union army. At first they were rejected, but after 1862 thousands were enlisted. Many would lose their lives in the war.

As the Union armies moved into Confederate territories, hundreds of runaway slaves flocked behind Union lines. Initially they were declared "contraband of war" and put into camps, but as the war continued, they provided vital support services.

In all, some 200,000 black American men and women worked for the Northern war effort as cooks, laborers, nurses, scouts, and spies.

THE END OF SLAVERY

Black leaders such as Frederick Douglass, who enlisted in 1863, saw the war as a means of freeing slaves.

But emancipation presented a political problem for Lincoln. Although slavery was banned in the North, racism was widespread. Northerners were worried that emancipation would mean an influx of vast numbers of Southern blacks. Lincoln was also worried about angering border states that were loyal to the Union, but committed to slavery. And finally, the US Constitution itself recognized slavery.

In 1862 Lincoln issued an order to free all slaves in states that had seceded from the Union. The official Emancipation Proclamation came into force on January 1, 1863.

The 54th Massachusetts Volunteers go into action during the Civil War.

LANDMARK DATES

1861 Confederate troops attack Fort Sumter; Civil War begins; Confiscation Act: any property used against the US to belong to the country; slaves were considered "property" and therefore would be free.

1862 Congress passes Contraband Act. Runaway slaves are classified as "contraband of war"; US Congress approves enlistment of freed blacks.

1863 Emancipation Proclamation comes into force; eight black regiments take part in assault on Fort Hudson, Louisiana; 54th Massachusetts Volunteers storm Fort Wagner.

1864 Congress announces equal pay and equipment for black soldiers.

1865 Civil War ends; Congress passes the 13th Amendment to the Constitution, outlawing slavery forever.

It announced that slaves in rebellious states "would be forever free."
It did not include slave states loyal to the Union. Two years later, the war ended with a Union victory. Slavery was abolished throughout the US—after 250 years it had finally come to an end.

BLACK SOLDIERS

Between 1863 and 1865 some 186,000 black Americans served in the Union Army.

About 20,000 served in the Union Navy. There were 166 all-black regiments, mostly commanded by white officers. Only 100 black Americans became officers.

At first there was considerable racial prejudice against black soldiers. They received poorer rations and medical supplies than white soldiers, and only half their pay—$7 a month, compared with $13.

Eventually they gained equal pay and conditions. One of the best-known black regiments was the 54th Massachusetts Volunteers, the first black regiment raised in the North.

Soldiers of the 54th fought bravely at the storming of Fort Wagner in Charleston Harbor, South Carolina. Their bravery helped overcome Northern prejudice.

Reconstruction

In 1865 the US began the task of reconstruction. Slavery was over and civil rights were introduced. But whites in the South soon began a campaign of terror against black people. And racial segregation was enshrined in law.

AFTERMATH

By the end of the Civil War the Southern states were devastated. One by one they were readmitted to the Union. Blacks in the South were finally free. Families were reunited. But, as Frederick Douglass warned, the end of slavery did not mean the end of the struggle. Former slaves hoped to receive land but rarely did.

WASHINGTON

Booker T. Washington (1856–1915) was born into slavery. He was educated at Hampton Institute, one of the black schools set up during Reconstruction. He believed that for black people to advance, they had to do "useful work."

He thought black people should have practical training, as well as learning to read and write. He set up the Tuskegee Institute in 1881 and was its first principal. Some black leaders, such as W. E. B. Du Bois, disagreed with Washington because he worked with Southern whites.

Most traded slavery for sharecropping, toiling for white plantation owners for a share of the crop, rather than for wages.

Abraham Lincoln was assassinated in 1865. The new president was Tennessee-born Andrew Jackson. He believed that "white men alone" should govern. Even so, in 1866 Congress, which was controlled by radical Republicans, granted black Americans full citizenship, including the right to vote— at this time only men had the vote. Federal troops occupied the Southern states and forced them to allow black men to vote.

RECONSTRUCTION

During Reconstruction (1866–77), the government tried to rebuild the South and guarantee black civil rights. By 1867 there were 735,000 black voters in the South.

In South Carolina a few black men were elected to public office. The Freedman's Bureau, a federal agency, was set up in 1865 to help ex-slaves find work and provide education and training.

Northern educators and members of the black clergy set up schools throughout the South. At first most teachers were white, but by 1870 about one-third were black.

The drive for education also led to the founding of the first black colleges. Between 1865 and 1877 nearly 50 black colleges were set up. These schools were often overcrowded, but they gave Southern black Americans their first chance for higher education.

JIM CROW ERA

White Southerners resented these changes. When Northern officials left in 1877, they regained control of state governments and introduced the so-called Jim Crow Laws.

These banned black people from white schools, restaurants, public transportation, and housing, creating a segregation of races that continued until the 1960s.

Some whites launched a campaign of violence and intimidation against black people. One of the most sinister and brutal organizations was the Ku Klux Klan. Formed in 1867, its members terrorized the South, whipping, lynching, and burning black people. Between 1880 and 1930 more than 3,000 were killed.

BLACKS LOSE THE VOTE

During the 1890s Southern states made voting dependent on literacy, property ownership, or a poll tax. This put black people at a disadvantage. In 1896 a famous court case declared the Jim Crow laws constitutional, and in 1898 the US Supreme Court upheld these disenfranchisement laws.

Thus, within 30 years of the end of the Civil War and Emancipation, black civil rights had been seriously undermined.

Hooded to prevent recognition, Ku Klux Klan members meet during the 1920s.

Black Nationalism

In the early 1900s black Americans challenged racial segregation. Some wanted integration; others, like Marcus Garvey, argued for black separatism. Thousands of black Americans left the South and a vibrant African-American culture emerged.

"I, too, am America."

Langston Hughes, from the poem *Epilogue*

THE NAACP

One of the first to argue for full equality was William Edward Burghardt Du Bois, the first black person to be awarded a PhD from Harvard University.

Du Bois and other activists met at Niagara Falls in 1905. Together they formed the Niagara Movement to campaign for all aspects of black civil rights.

In 1909 members of the Niagara Movement formed the National Association for the Advancement of Colored People (NAACP). Du Bois, who was the only black NAACP leader, produced its newspaper *Crisis*.

The NAACP's aims were to end segregation and to work for equal education and voting rights through the legal system, by bringing cases of discrimination to court.

BACK TO AFRICA

Not all blacks wanted integration with white people. An important element in their struggle was black nationalism.

Just as white slave owners had justified racism by saying that Africans were inferior, black nationalists now argued that it was white people who were inferior. They said African Americans should be take pride in and celebrate their African roots.

An NAACP meeting of the 1920s.

GARVEY

Marcus Garvey (1882–1940) was born in Jamaica. An influential black leader, Garvey called for a "back to Africa" movement in which people of African descent would settle in Liberia, Africa, and build a black state.

A flamboyant man, his vision, stirring speeches, and newspaper *Negro World* attracted millions of followers worldwide. He invested in a fleet of ships—the Black Star Steamship Line—to transport black Americans to Africa. He was criticized by black leaders such as W. E. B. Du Bois for his controversial views.

Marcus Garvey led this movement. He urged black Americans to create a separate black nation in Africa. In 1914 he founded the Universal Negro Improvement Association (UNIA). It gained support, and by 1916 there were more than 1,000 branches in several countries.

Through the efforts of Garvey and other leaders such as Edward Blyden, who wrote *African Life and Customs* (1908), black Americans gained a sense of purpose. Garvey's ideas were adopted by black leaders of the 1960s.

GREAT MIGRATION

After World War I (1914–18) agriculture in the US collapsed. Half a million black Americans left the South, driven out by lynchings, segregation, police brutality, and poverty. They migrated to northern industrial cities, such as Detroit, Chicago, and Cleveland in search of work and a better life.

Although conditions were better, racial prejudice existed in these cities too. There were race riots in Washington and Chicago, and racial segregation existed in many public places.

Some black people settled in the Harlem section of New York. During the 1920s and 1930s there was an upsurge of black literature, music, and theater, which became known as the Harlem Renaissance. Artists like Paul Robeson expressed their experiences through their work.

Jazz musicians also came north, to Chicago and New York, and people flocked to places like the Cotton Club. But even great performers like Bessie Smith and Billie Holiday faced terrible racial prejudice.

HARLEM RENAISSANCE

• 1916 Apollo Theater opens in Harlem. Many black entertainers begin careers there.

• 1917 Writer James Weldon Johnson publishes *Fifty Years and Other Poems*

• 1921 Eubie Blake and Noble Sissle write and produce *Shuffle Along*, the first black musical; Paul Robeson and Charles Gilpin appear in O'Neill's play *Emperor Jones*

• 1922 Poet Claude McKay publishes *Harlem Shadows*; Cotton Club opens.

• 1923 Blues singer Bessie Smith records "Down Hearted Blues"; dancer Josephine Baker makes stage debut in *Chocolate Dandies*

• 1924 Paul Robeson makes screen debut in *Body and Soul*

• 1926 Poet Langston Hughes publishes *Weary Blues*

• 1931 Katherine Dunham creates modern dance style combining ballet and African symbolism.

• 1932 Dancer Bill "Bojangles" Robinson stars in *Harlem is Heaven*, the first all-black talking movie.

Civil Rights

In the late 1950s a massive civil rights movement emerged that would transform the lives of black Americans. Under the leadership of Martin Luther King Jr., it ended the entrenched racial segregation of the South and achieved major civil rights legislation.

"I have a dream . . ."

Martin Luther King Jr., August 28, 1963

EARLY STEPS

Some progress had been made. Black Americans fought for their country during World War II (1939–45), and in 1948 President Truman ended segregation in the armed forces.

NAACP lawyers continued to bring cases before the Supreme Court. In 1954, in the case of *Brown v. Board of Education of Topeka, Kansas*, the Supreme Court ruled that separate educational facilities were unequal and unconstitutional.

In spite of this, white Southerners still resisted integration. In 1957 black teenagers tried to register at Central High, Little Rock, Arkansas. They were not allowed to do so. President Eisenhower had to send troops to escort them in to school.

BUS BOYCOTT

In 1955 Rosa Parks, a former NAACP secretary, was arrested for refusing to move to the black section of a bus in Montgomery, Alabama. In protest, black women began a bus boycott.

A new black leader, Martin Luther King Jr., a Baptist minister, came to prominence. Under his direction, the boycott continued, and a year later bus segregation in Alabama came to an end.

GATHERING MOMENTUM

Other facilities in the South still remained closed to blacks. With King at its head, the civil rights movement gathered momentum. King and other black ministers formed the Southern Christian Leadership Conference (SCLC) to achieve integration through nonviolent tactics. Grass-roots groups were set up, including the Congress of Racial Equality (CORE) and the Student Non-Violent Coordinating Committee (SNCC).

Civil rights activists—both black and white—used various tactics to force change.

These included boycotts and sit-ins, when black activists deliberately sat in places reserved for whites. In 1961 CORE launched "freedom rides" to break down segregation on interstate transportation outside Alabama.

White reaction was often violent. Martin Luther King's home was firebombed and some 3,600 freedom riders were arrested. Black activists were harassed, beaten, imprisoned, and murdered, and their homes were burned.

The movement reached a climax in 1963 when King led more than 250,000 people on a march to Washington, D.C., where he gave his powerful "I have a dream" speech. President John F. Kennedy had already tried and failed to get a new civil rights bill through Congress.

In 1964, following Kennedy's assassination, and with pressure from President Lyndon Johnson, the bill was made law.

The most far-reaching civil rights bill in US history, it finally outlawed any form of racial discrimination.

It also protected an individual's right to employment, the vote, and access to public places.

KING

Martin Luther King Jr. (1929–68) was a charismatic black Baptist minister. Leader of the civil rights movement from the mid-1950s, he devoted his life to achieving equality and freedom for black Americans. He was influenced by the nonviolent tactics of the Indian leader Mahatma Gandhi and urged his followers to use similar methods. Born and educated in Atlanta, Georgia, King trained to be a doctor but entered the ministry. In 1953 he married Coretta Scott, and by 1955 had become a respected black leader. In 1964 he was awarded the Nobel Peace Prize. King faced constant death threats. He was assassinated in 1968.

Black Power

In 1965 Congress passed the Voting Rights Act. Integration was slow and met violent resistance. Some black activists, angered by the slow pace of change, broke away; black power was born.

"Black is beautiful"
Black power slogan

VOTER REGISTRATION
The Civil Rights Act had outlawed racial segregation. But in much of the South black people were still barred from voting.

In February 1965 a black activist campaigning for voter registration was murdered in Alabama. Martin Luther King and other black leaders organized a march from Selma to Montgomery. Twice, state troopers, armed with billy clubs and tear gas, attacked the peaceful protest. Eventually the National Guard was called in and 50,000 supporters, black and white, joined the march. Within days, President Johnson got the Voting Rights Act through Congress.

In 1967 the attorney general sent federal agents to the South to register black voters. The number of black voters increased dramatically.

BLACK MUSLIMS
Martin Luther King continued to campaign against social injustice and black poverty. In 1968 he was organizing a "Poor People's Campaign" when he was shot in Memphis. His death caused shock, grief, and anger. Black people rioted; a second Civil Rights Act was passed.

But even before his death, divisions had appeared in the civil rights movement. Not all black activists supported King's nonviolent stance. A new black nationalism had emerged in the 1950s which had its origins in the Nation of Islam, founded in 1929.

Activist Stokely Carmichael addresses a black power rally.

The Black Muslims rejected all aspects of white America. Unlike King, who wanted integration, Black Muslims wanted complete separation from whites.

Their greatest leader and spokesman was Malcolm X. Like Garvey before him, Malcolm X celebrated blackness. Throughout the '50s and '60s he had a huge following.

BLACK POWER

Young activists such as Stokely Carmichael and Angela Davis—both SNCC members—were influenced by Malcolm X.

Like him, they rejected the non-violent tactics of the established civil rights movement. They wanted to fight back and argued that "black power" should be used against white oppressors. In 1968 the SNCC officially broke away from the established civil rights movement.

In 1966 Huey Newton and Bobby Seale founded the Black Panthers. They supported the use of guns and advocated violent revolution to achieve black liberation.

The Panthers set up clinics and free food programs in the black ghettos. But their militant tactics—there were several shootouts between Panthers and the police—alienated them from both white and black people.

In the late 1960s the Panthers began to work with white radical groups. By the mid-1970s the Panthers and the black power movement were declining, but they had reinforced black consciousness and pride.

FACT FILE

BLACK POWER

1952 Malcolm X released from prison.

1963 Civil rights protests, Birmingham, Alabama. Troops use dogs and water cannons against protesters. White racists bomb a Baptist church. Four young black women killed.

1965 Voting Rights Act bans literacy and other tests that disenfranchise black voters; Malcolm X assassinated in Harlem, New York; race riots in the Watts area of Los Angeles leave 34 dead, 900 injured.

1966 SNCC adopts "black power" slogan; Black Panther Party formed; race riots in Chicago, New York, and Cleveland.

1967 Black power conference, Newark, New Jersey, advocates partitioning US into two nations—white and black.

1968 Martin Luther King assassinated; black American medal winners give black power clenched-fist salute at Olympic Games, Mexico City.

MALCOLM X

Malcolm X (1925–65) was an influential black leader. In 1931 his father was found dead. Malcolm believed white racists were responsible. In 1946 he was imprisoned for burglary, and in prison he became a Black Muslim. After his release he adopted the letter "X" as a last name, symbol of the unknown African name of his slave ancestors. A fiery speaker, he believed in black separatism and rejected nonviolence, urging blacks to win their freedom "by any means necessary." He split with the Black Muslims and, in 1964, founded the Organization of Afro-American Unity to promote black nationalism. He was assassinated in Harlem in 1965.

The 21st Century

Black Americans have achieved much in their fight for equality. They have made their mark in every field from politics to entertainment. But poverty is greater among black Americans than whites, and prejudice remains. The struggle for true equality continues.

AFFIRMATIVE ACTION

In 1965 the government adopted "affirmative action" to try to ensure that black Americans received an equal chance in employment and education. Equal opportunity programs were introduced to put black people first in terms of job applications, admissions to school, and so on. Such programs were later introduced for women and other disadvantaged groups.

Increasing numbers of black people were recruited by colleges and employers. But not everyone agreed with affirmative action. Some argued that it was a kind of reverse discrimination; others said it was absolutely necessary. There were legal challenges. In the late 1990s affirmative action was ruled unconstitutional in most cases.

POLITICAL POWER

By 1971 62 percent of eligible black people in the South had been registered to vote, compared with only 20 percent in 1960. Black voters were a small percentage of the total vote, but politicians could no longer ignore them.

Since 1970 the number of black elected officials has increased. In 1970 there were 48 black mayors; in 1990 there were 314.

Black mayors in significant cities included Harold Washington in Chicago, Sharon Pratt Kelley in Washington, D.C., and David Dinkins in New York.

The number of black people in Congress also increased, from 10 in 1970 to 26 in 1990. Black candidates, such as Jesse Jackson, made serious bids to achieve the presidency.

AFRICAN-AMERICAN CULTURE

Africans arrived in the Americas with Europeans, so African-American culture is part of American culture. It draws on African roots, the Caribbean, the American Deep South, and urban experiences.

MORRISON

The writer Toni Morrison (1931–) has done much to further African-American literature. She was born in Ohio. Her parents had been sharecroppers in the South. Morrison writes about the African-American experience, particularly the efforts of black Americans to survive. Her novels include *Sula* (1973), which describes poor black Southerners, *Song of Solomon* (1977), and *Beloved* (1987), the moving account of a former slave haunted by the ghost of her beloved daughter whom she killed rather than see her become a slave. In 1993, Morrison was awarded the Nobel Prize for Literature.

Presidential candidate Jesse Jackson addresses a rally.

Music may be the area where African Americans have made the best-known contributions. Jazz, gospel, blues, rock, and, most recently, rap originate in the black experience. Musicians like Miles Davis and opera singer Jessye Norman have achieved superstardom.

In movies and television too, African Americans have made huge contributions. Stars such as Sidney Poitier and Oprah Winfrey and filmmakers like Spike Lee have become famous.

African-American writers such as Alice Walker, Maya Angelou, and Toni Morrison have drawn on their experiences as black women to create dramatic writing that is now receiving world recognition.

POPULATION AND DISCRIMINATION

In 1990 there were nearly 30 million African Americans in the US—about 12 percent of the population. Most black Americans live in major cities such as New York, Detroit, Chicago, and Los Angeles.

States with the highest percentage of black Americans are former slave-owning states such as South Carolina (30 percent) and Alabama (27 percent).

Black Americans have achieved equality within the law. But, on the average, the income of black American families is still well behind that of white families. Infant mortality is also higher. African Americans still have to fight to achieve full equality.

Glossary

abolitionist Man or woman who campaigned to abolish or end slavery.

affirmative action Policies intended to increase the number of people from certain groups, such as black people or women, in jobs, education, government, etc.

amendment A change, usually to a document. In US law an amendment is a change or addition made to the Constitution.

boycott Refusing to handle or use goods or services. For example, some Americans boycotted stores and restaurants that did not want to serve black people.

Black Muslims Members of an all-black religious movement in the US called the Nation of Islam. Members considered whites "devils" and argued for separation of blacks and whites.

colony A place in one country that is settled and governed by another country. The settlers in the colony come from the "mother" country and are called colonists.

Congress The national lawmaking body of the United States, made up of elected members. It comprises the House of Representatives and the Senate.

constitution Legal document that sets out the laws and rights of a country's citizens.

cotton gin Machine invented by Eli Whitney in 1793 to separate cotton from its seeds. It had fine teeth that "combed" the plant.

discrimination Different treatment because of prejudice about sex, race, or ability. Racial discrimination is treating someone differently because of his or her race.

emancipation Freedom from slavery.

freedom rides Tactic for desegregating buses. Members of the Congress of Racial Equality (CORE) sent white and black activists to sit together on interstate buses, deliberately flouting the law.

infant mortality The number of children who die before the age of one.

integration Bringing together people who have previously been separated or segregated; for example, black and white students attending the same school.

Jim Crow Laws Laws that imposed racial segregation in the Southern states of the USA between 1877 and the 1950s. Probably named after a character in a minstrel show.

lynching	Mob violence during which someone is killed, usually by hanging. A method of intimidation used against black people by the Ku Klux Klan.
manumission	To set a slave free. It means literally to "free from the hand."
maroons	African slaves who lived in the forests of Jamaica. In 1738 the British made a peace treaty with the maroons, giving them their freedom.
Middle Passage	The crossing of the slave ships from Africa to the Americas.
nationalism	Political movement that seeks to unify a country. Black nationalism sought to unify black people by urging them to be proud of their African roots. Some black nationalists wanted to set up a free state for African Americans in Africa.
Negro	Black person of African origin. Often considered offensive, the term is now usually replaced by the word "black."
New World	Term used by European colonizers to describe the Americas.
plantation	Large farm where crops such as sugar, tobacco, or cotton were grown. Plantations were worked by slave labor.
racism	Prejudice about one particular race. A belief that one race is superior to another, usually that whites are superior to blacks. Discrimination based on that belief.
Reconstruction	Period after the Civil War when the government was "reconstructing" the South.
secede	Withdraw formally, for example when the Southern states seceded from the Union.
segregation	Separation. Racial segregation keeps people of different races apart from each other.
sexism	Belief that one sex, or gender, is better than another.
sharecropper	A plantation worker who was paid with a share of the crop or harvest.
sit-ins	Tactic used by black civil rights activists who deliberately sat in places reserved for whites, for example in restaurants and on public transportation.
slave	A person who is regarded and treated as the property of another person, often by law.
suffrage	The right to vote in political elections.
Union	The states that did not secede, and remained part of the United States. During the Civil War the Northern states were referred to as the "Union" states.

PICTURE CREDITS

Corbis: 22b.
Wally McNamee/Corbis: 29t.
Board & Trustees of the National Museums and Galleries on Merseyside/AKG London: 7c.
Peter Newark's Historical Pictures: 8-9c, 10-11b, 16-17b, 19t.
North Wind Pictures: 12t.
Flip Schulke/Corbis: 26b.
Underwood & Underwood/AKG London: 20-21b.
While every attempt has been made to clear copyright, should there be any inadvertent omission please apply to the publisher regarding rectification.